FARMERS, FIREFIGHTERS, AND TEACHERS
THEY ARE NOUNS!

By LINDA AYERS

Illustrated by DAVID BUCS

Music Arranged and Produced by
MUSICAL YOUTH PRODUCTIONS

CANTATA
LEARNING

WWW.CANTATALEARNING.COM

CANTATA LEARNING

Published by Cantata Learning
1710 Roe Crest Drive
North Mankato, MN 56003
www.cantatalearning.com

A note to educators and librarians from the publisher: Cantata Learning has provided the following data to assist in book processing and suggested use of Cantata Learning product.

Publisher's Cataloging-in-Publication Data
Prepared by Librarian Consultant: Ann-Marie Begnaud
Library of Congress Control Number: 2015958164
    Farmers, Firefighters, and Teachers : They Are Nouns!
    Series: Read, Sing, Learn : Songs about the Parts of Speech
    By Linda Ayers
    Illustrated by David Bucs
    Summary: A song about nouns and the fall season.
    ISBN: 978-1-63290-588-8 (library binding/CD)
    ISBN: 978-1-63290-572-7 (paperback/CD)
Suggested Dewey and Subject Headings:
    Dewey: E 428
    LCSH Subject Headings: English language – Grammar – Juvenile literature. | Autumn – Juvenile literature. | English language – Grammar – Songs and music – Texts. | Autumn – Songs and music – Texts. | English language – Grammar – Juvenile sound recordings. | Autumn – Juvenile sound recordings.
    Sears Subject Headings: English language – Parts of speech. | Seasons. | School songbooks. | Children's songs. | World music.
    BISAC Subject Headings: JUVENILE NONFICTION / Language Arts / Grammar. | JUVENILE NONFICTION / Music Songbooks. | JUVENILE NONFICTION / Concepts / Seasons.

Book design and art direction, Tim Palin Creative
Editorial direction, Flat Sole Studio
Music direction, Elizabeth Draper
Music arranged and produced by Musical Youth Productions

Printed in the United States of America in North Mankato, Minnesota.
072016   0335CGF16

What is a **noun**? It's a person, place, or thing. That means you, your school, and the bicycle you pedal around on are nouns. What sort of nouns do you see around you?

To find out more about nouns, turn the page and sing a song about the fall season!

Farmers and firefighters
and teachers in our town.
They're **community** helpers.
They're people, and they're nouns.

Nouns are people, places, animals, and things,
like teachers, schools, squirrels, and pumpkins.

Nouns are a part of **speech**.

We need them when we sing and when we speak.

The fields and the **orchards**
are growing all around.
They're where we go on field trips.
They're places, and they're nouns.

Nouns are people, places, animals, and things,
like teachers, schools, squirrels, and pumpkins.

Nouns are a part of speech.

We need them when we sing and when we speak.

Geese and monarch butterflies
in fall are southern bound,
while squirrels gather nuts.
They're animals, and they're nouns.

Nouns are people, places, animals, and things,
like teachers, schools, squirrels, and pumpkins.

Nouns are a part of speech.

We need them when we sing and when we speak.

Scarecrows and pumpkins,
and leaves of orange and brown,
decorate fall **holidays**.
They're things, and they're nouns.

Nouns are people, places, animals, and things,
like teachers, schools, squirrels, and pumpkins.

Nouns are a part of speech.

We need them when we sing and when we speak.

SONG LYRICS
Farmers, Firefighters, and Teachers

Farmers and firefighters
and teachers in our town.
They're community helpers.
They're people, and they're nouns.

Nouns are people, places, animals, and things,
like teachers, schools, squirrels, and pumpkins.

Nouns are a part of speech.
We need them when we sing and when we speak.

The fields and the orchards
are growing all around.
They're where we go on field trips.
They're places, and they're nouns.

Nouns are people, places, animals, and things,
like teachers, schools, squirrels, and pumpkins.

Nouns are a part of speech.
We need them when we sing and when we speak.

Geese and monarch butterflies
in fall are southern bound,
while squirrels gather nuts.
They're animals, and they're nouns.

Nouns are people, places, animals, and things,
like teachers, schools, squirrels, and pumpkins.

Nouns are a part of speech.
We need them when we sing and when we speak.

Scarecrows and pumpkins,
and leaves of orange and brown,
decorate fall holidays.
They're things, and they're nouns.

Nouns are people, places, animals, and things,
like teachers, schools, squirrels, and pumpkins.

Nouns are a part of speech.
We need them when we sing and when we speak.

Farmers, Firefighters, and Teachers

Indie Pop (Folk/World)
Musical Youth Productions

Verse 1, 2

1. Farm - ers and fire - fight-ers and teach - ers in our town. They're com - mu - ni - ty help - ers. They're peo - ple, and they're nouns.

Chorus

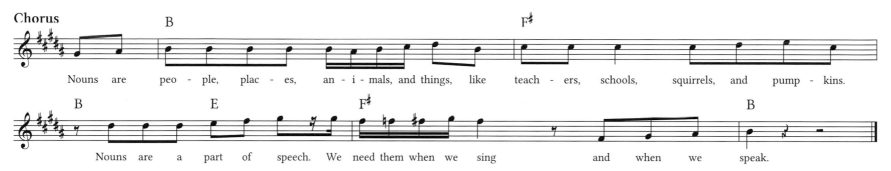

Nouns are peo - ple, plac - es, an - i - mals, and things, like teach - ers, schools, squirrels, and pump - kins.

Nouns are a part of speech. We need them when we sing and when we speak.

Verse 2

The fields and the orchards
are growing all around.
They're where we go on field trips.
They're places, and they're nouns.

Chorus

Bridge

Geese and mon - arch but-ter-flies in fall are south - ern bound, while squirrels gath - er nuts. They're an - i - mals, and they're nouns.

Chorus

Verse 3

Scare - crows and pump - kins, and leaves of orange and brown, dec - o - rate fall hol - i - days. They're things, and they're nouns.

Chorus

23

GLOSSARY

community—a group of people who live in the same area

holiday—a day of celebration

noun—a word that names a person, place, or thing

orchards—fields or farms where fruit trees are grown

speech—spoken language

GUIDED READING ACTIVITIES

1. Look at the illustration on pages 6 and 7. How do each of the people shown help their community?

2. Carving pumpkins into jack-o'-lanterns is a fun part of fall. Draw a picture of how you would carve a jack-o'-lantern.

3. The children on pages 10 and 11 are going on a field trip. Have you ever been on a field trip? What did you do?

TO LEARN MORE

Blaisdell, Bette. *A Pocket Full of Nouns*. North Mankato, MN: Capstone Press, 2014.

Felix, Rebecca. *Can You Be a Bee?* Mankato, MN: Amicus, 2015.

Johnson, Robin. *The Word Wizard's Book of Nouns*. New York: Crabtree Publishing Company, 2015.

Murray, Kara. *Nouns and Pronouns*. New York: PowerKids Press, 2014.